# COLOR YOURSELF INSPIRED

# Everyday Blessings

# COLORING BOOK

## SPIRITUAL REFRESHMENT
## FOR WOMEN

Print ISBN 978-1-68322-098-5

Scripture quotations are taken from the New Life Version copyright © 1969 and 2003. Used by permission of Barbour Publishing, Inc., Uhrichsville, Ohio, 44683. All rights reserved.

Cover illustration: Emma Segal
Interior illustrations: Traci Bixby, Elisa Paganelli, Carol Robinson, Emma Segal, Nicky Storr

Published by Barbour Books, an imprint of Barbour Publishing, Inc., P.O. Box 719, Uhrichsville, OH 44683, www.barbourbooks.com.

*Our mission is to publish and distribute inspirational products offering exceptional value and biblical encouragement to the masses.*

Member of the
Evangelical Christian
Publishers Association

Printed in the United States of America.

COLOR YOURSELF INSPIRED

# Everyday Blessings COLORING BOOK

## SPIRITUAL REFRESHMENT FOR WOMEN

BARBOUR BOOKS

An Imprint of Barbour Publishing, Inc.

WHATEVER IS GOOD
AND PERFECT
COMES TO US
FROM GOD.

(JAMES 1:17)

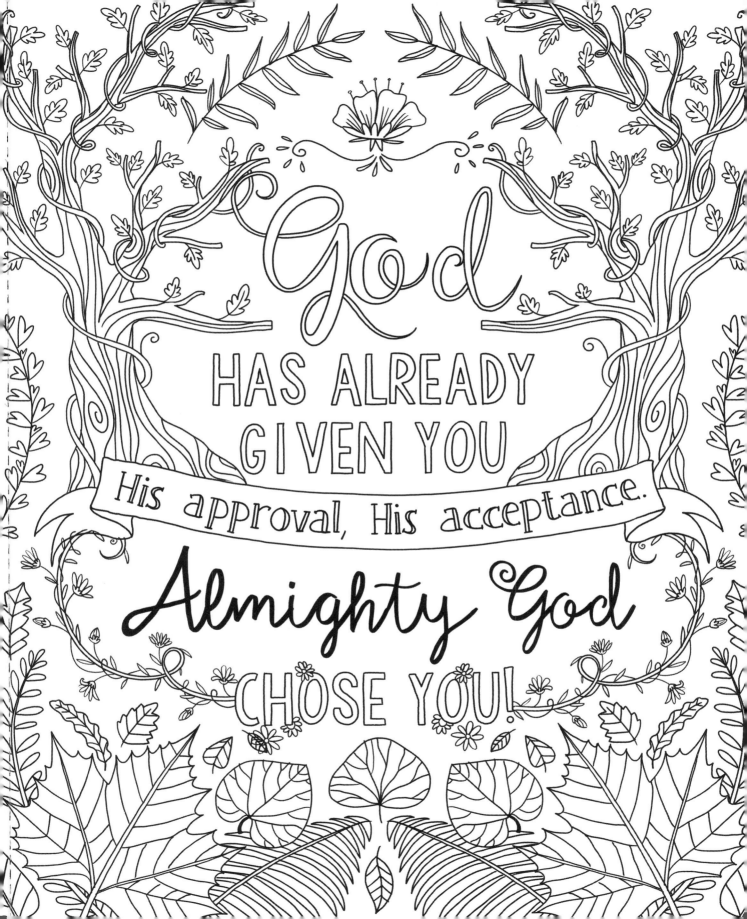

EVEN BEFORE THE WORLD WAS MADE, God chose us for Himself BECAUSE of His love.

(EPHESIANS 1:4)

WORK TO BE
*as fully beautiful*
AS GOD CREATED
YOU TO BE.

your beauty should come from the inside. It should come from the heart.

(1 PETER 3:4)

**LOOK** to Jesus. His loving character never changes. He was, is, and will always **BE.**

Jesus Christ is the same yesterday and today and forever.

Hebrews 13:8

Listen to the Lord; Choose him.

Place
your hope
in God's goodness.

God's word gives us strength and hope.

Romans 15:4

I HAVE learned to be HAPPY with whatever I HAVE.

Philippians 4:11

JARDIN

Beneath the soil,
God tends your faith—
the longer you
walk with Him,
the deeper His
hold on you.

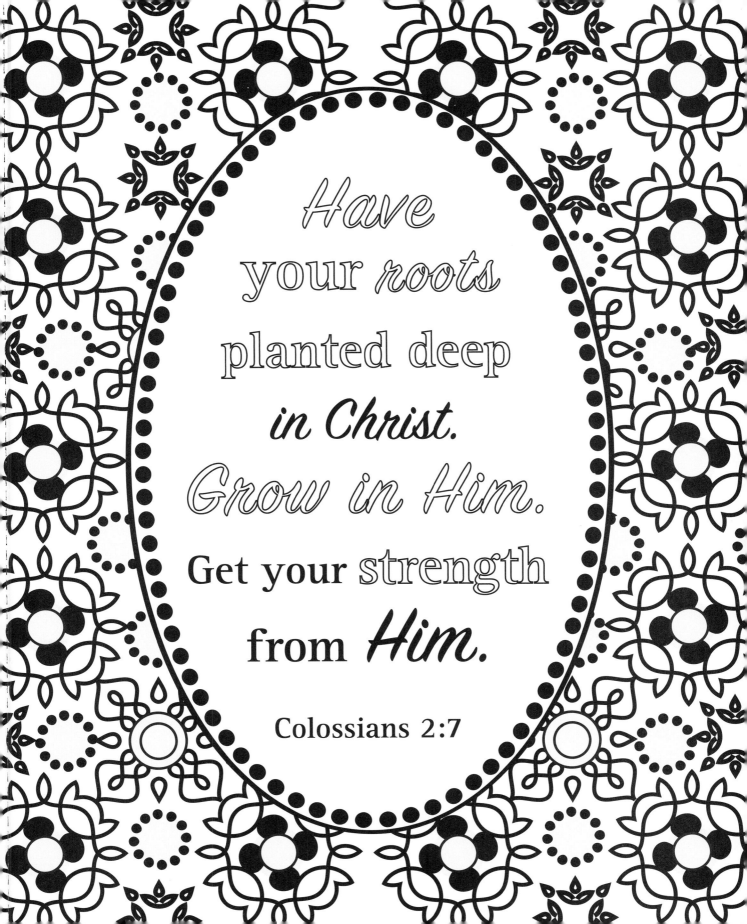

Open every door wide... and invite GOD in.

Keep my life,

for I am faithful to You.

You are my God.

Psalm 86:2

God hears. He's always listening, always encouraging.

I love the Lord,
because He
hears my voice
and my prayers.

Psalm 116:1

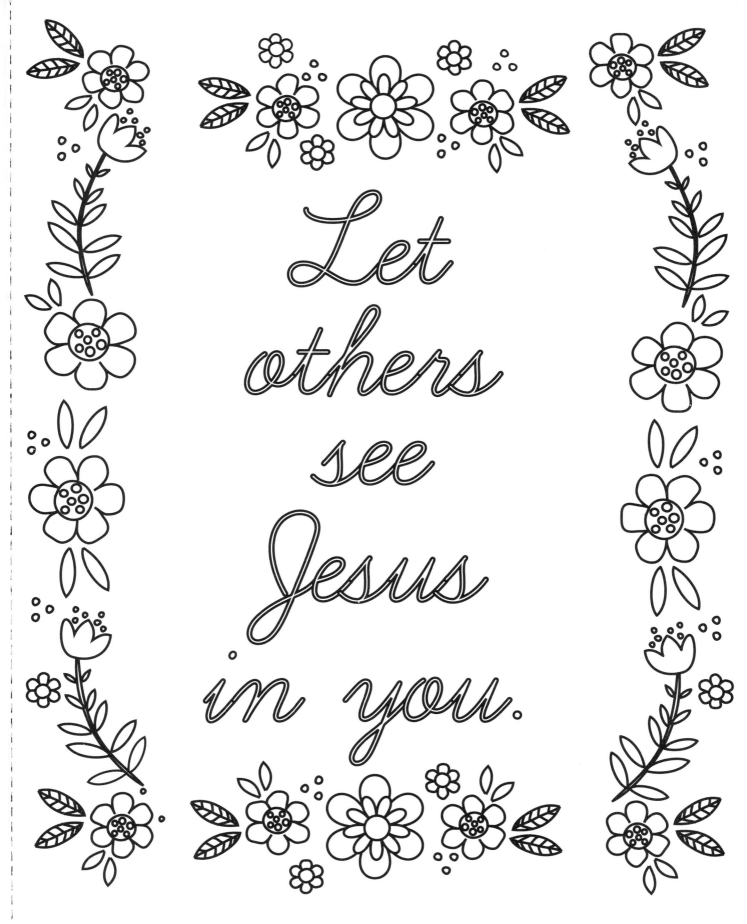

You
are God's children...
You
are to shine
as lights.

Philippians 2:15

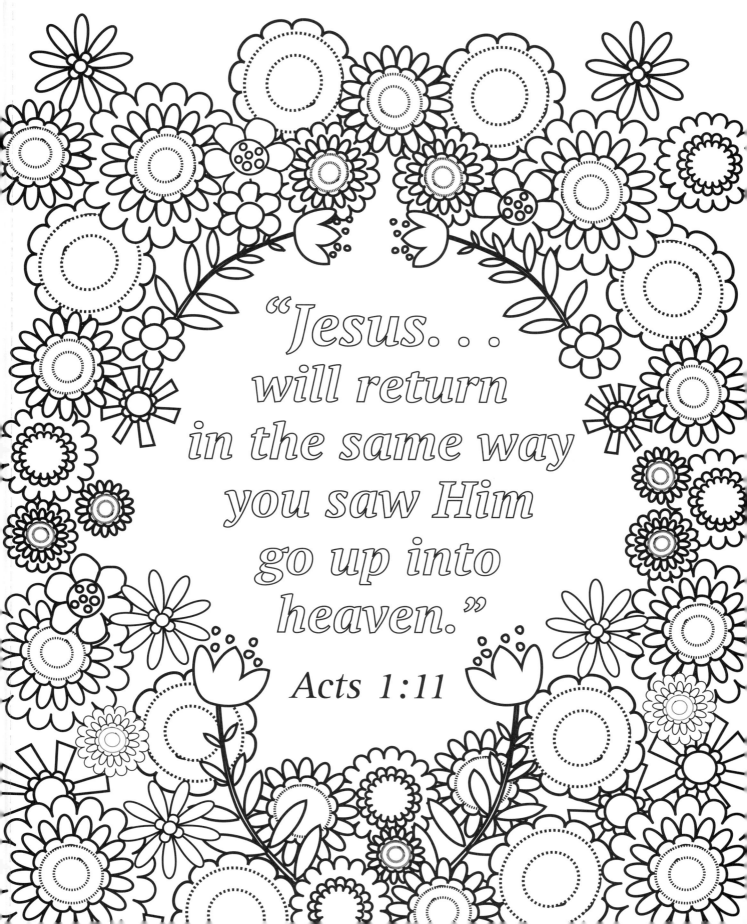

"Jesus. . . will return in the same way you saw Him go up into heaven."

Acts 1:11

"I HAVE FORGIVEN YOU FOR ALL THAT YOU HAVE DONE,"

SAYS THE LORD GOD. ~ EZEKIEL 16:63

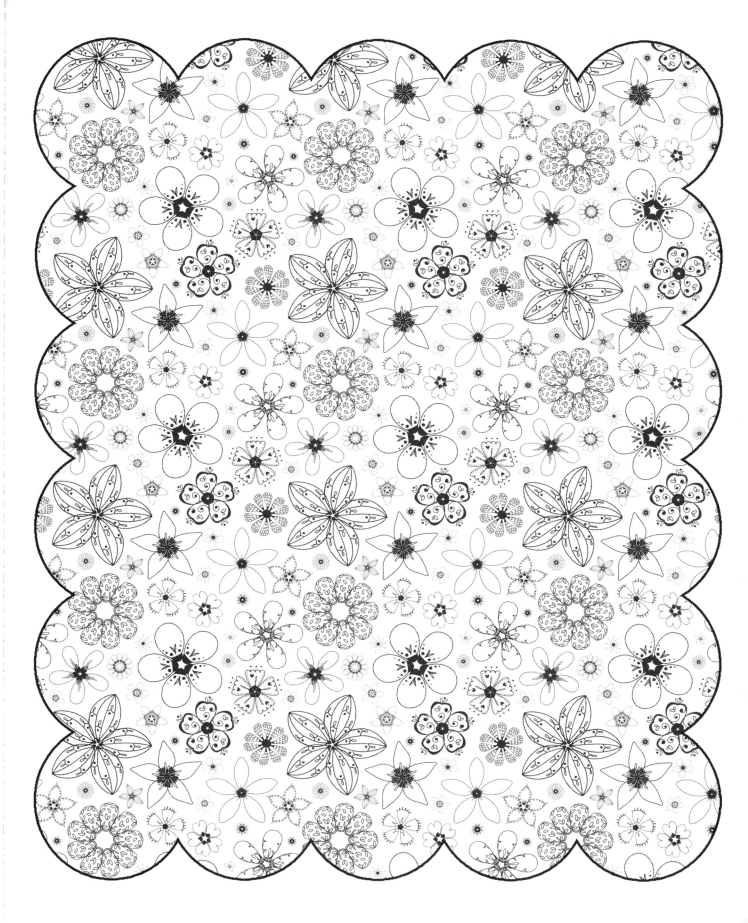

"FOR I KNOW THE PLANS I HAVE FOR YOU, PLANS FOR WELL-BEING AND NOT FOR TROUBLE, TO GIVE YOU A FUTURE AND A HOPE"

JEREMIAH 29:11